I AM FOUR STONES

ATHELYN DANIEL

Authors Tranquility Press
ATLANTA, GEORGIA

Copyright © 2023 by Athelyn Daniel.

All rights reserved. No part of this publication may be reproduced, distributed or transmitted in any form or by any means, including photocopying, recording, or other electronic or mechanical methods, without the prior written permission of the publisher, except in the case of brief quotations embodied in critical reviews and certain other noncommercial uses permitted by copyright law. For permission requests, write to the publisher, addressed "Attention: Permissions Coordinator," at the address below.

Athelyn Daniel/Author's Tranquility Press
3800 CAMP CREEK PKWY SW BLDG 1400-116 #1255
Atlanta, GA 30331
www.authorstranquilitypress.com

Ordering Information:
Quantity sales. Special discounts are available on quantity purchases by corporations, associations, and others. For details, contact the "Special Sales Department" at the address above.

I am Four Stones/Athelyn Daniel
Paperback: 978-1-960675-18-7
eBook: 978-1-958179-58-1

FOUR STONES

FOREWORD

"It is very difficult for a child to aspire to and become what they have never seen. To be able to imbue within a child a vision of purpose, integrity, undaunted determination and the possibility of achieving the seemingly impossible that transcends their present living environment, heredity, gender, and all other obstacles is a challenge. "FOUR STONES" is the example that demonstrates and, testifies to a Loving and Caring Family rearing a child that overcomes all."

Pastor Cleophas C. Mim is a former Combat Medic, recipient of The Silver Star, Purple Heart, three Bronze Stars, Army Commendation Medal w/"V", U.S. Army Reserves Chaplain, Hospital Chaplain, Sworn Police Chaplain, Church Pastor retired, and National Motivational Speaker.

**Dedicated
to
Athelyn South
my mother**

Start each day anew by being the best you.

Not seeking perfection that is a goal never conquered.

Perfection invites failure in recognizing what your best is.

Being the best at what you do is sustainable and satisfying.

One Sunday afternoon while waiting in my grandparent's backyard after church for my parents to pick me up, I discovered a loose board in the fence. This loose board provided an opening that would lead to the alley and then to the street. A portal to freedom at eight years old. I crawled through it, and I was alone in the alley behind the house. As children, my cousins and I played every weekend in the yard at my grandparents' home after church, however, we were not allowed out of my grandmother's yard unless an adult accompanied us. I wandered without fear down the alley to the street to the grocery store, two blocks away. Once inside the store, I stopped at the register where the candy was displayed. Excited and pleased with myself at my escape, I put a piece of candy in my mouth. I had intended to pay for the candy. I had my allowance in my pocket but before I could pay for it a voice said: "Aren't you one of Mother Jackson's grandchildren?" I said "NO" and ran out of the store without paying for the candy in my mouth.

I ran down the streets to the alley and back to the broken place in the fence at my grandmother's backyard and crawled back through the hole. I was immediately stopped inside by the feet of my father and grandmother blocking my way to the house. I began to cry out of fear and shame. I heard my father say, "Go get me a stone." I was frightened and confused, I had heard him say before "go get the belt" to be spanked or whipped. I had heard my grandmother say, "Go get me a stick or switch" to be spanked, but never a stone. Reluctantly, I walked over to retrieve a stone and returned with a hand-size stone. He said, "No, go get a big stone like the ones your grandmother uses as a wall for the flowers." Slowly, I walked to the wall, and I found a large flat stone that I struggled to bring back to him. I dropped the large, flat, heavy stone in front of my father and grandmother. My father said, "Stand on it, this is your foundation. This stone is like your Creator: solid, strong, unchanging, everlasting, and the only thing superior to you. Build your life on this stone."

THE FIRST STONE
FOUNDATION

"Go get another stone," he demanded. I stepped away toward the flowers to find another large stone and dragged it to my father and grandmother. He told me "This is your gender."

I did not know or understand what he meant. What is gender? I thought with this stone he will crush me for being disobedient and leaving the yard. Is this part of the punishment coming? I was shaking and crying. As if he read my thoughts, he told me your gender is - you are a female, a girl.

THE SECOND STONE

You will one day be a woman. You must respect and protect yourself, avoid putting yourself in unnecessary harm. As a woman, you will be the director and conductor of behavior, learning, and hope in your home. You will be the mother who teaches, loves, and cares for the children in your home. You will be the master of creativity for survival and the face of perseverance at work. You can be the source of strength in the community and a leader of your people. Women have unique responsibilities and significant roles in life. God loves women; they have a distinctive status in this world. God gave His only begotten Son to be born to a woman. God could have opened the heavens to have Jesus descend from the clouds to be among us. God could have unbolted the lightning and had Jesus appear majestically amongst the lightning with a flash and the roar of the thunder. God could have cracked a blow to puncture the earth and had Jesus emerge from the soil. Yet God delivered Him in the arms of a woman. Be aware of the wisdom of Jesus' mother who requested the first miracle, for she knew of His power. Remember the loyalty of the women who followed Jesus during the crucifixion, during His pain and affliction. A woman was last at the cross. A woman was first to see Jesus at the tomb and a woman told the disciples Jesus was not dead but resurrected. Respect yourself, and do not allow yourself to be disrespected

because of your behavior."

"Go get another stone," he bellowed. When I returned with the heavy stone, he said, "This stone represents your race. You can change your hair; braid it, curl it, straighten it, grow it, cut it, color it, shave it off or buy a wig. You can lose weight or gain weight. You can have plastic surgery to change your features and your shape. You can dress in expensive designer clothes, but you will still be seen first by your color. Before anyone knows who you are and what you are capable of, they will see your color. You were created to be magnificent, dressed and armored in this color. Exquisite according to the Creator not measured not by social standards. Whatever, others do or say of your race, uplift and respect your race, and yourself. Live in "your color" with joy."

THE THIRD STONE

My father paused then he continued: "Go get another stone." I went to the wall and pulled up another large stone wondering what else he was going to say or do. I returned for the fourth time hauling a heavy stone and placing it on the ground after which he sternly said, "This stone represents your family, your name. When you left this yard the family name was intact and respected. But you left the yard and you lied, you stole, you denied your name and your family. You must value your name and cherish the others that share it with you. You are to add to the worth of your name by the things you do to represent God, your gender, your race, your family citizen of earth. Be unmatched in character – "be four stones of faith, strength, influence, and uncompromised integrity."

THE FOURTH STONE

My grandmother handed me her cloth shopping bag and told me to place the stones inside the bag. When I finished forcing the stones into the bag, the bag was strained and torn. My hands were dirty, scratched and swollen. My father told me to pick up the bag. I attempted to pull up the heavy bag, but I failed. My father directed me to stoop down and lift the bag. My father and grandmother waited patiently while I wrestled to stand with the bag.

When I finally stood up with the bag in my arms he said, "You will keep these four stones with you for the rest of your life, be dedicated to their importance, and bear them wherever you go." Through my tears, I told him the bag was heavy and I couldn't carry the stones in the bag every day." My father touched my head and aimed his finger at my heart and said, "Carry the stones here."

Daily I carry four stones faith, color, gender, and family name. None of them are heavy.

They are what directs my actions.

As a child, I carried small stones in my pocket, as a remembrance of the day. Over the years, my family retold and reminded me of my role of being four stones. As time passed, I became conscious of the importance of the significance of honoring and being four stones.

Gradually, I understood the gift of the lesson taught that day. I now recognize how the lesson that Sunday afternoon shaped and clarified the worth and power of my being. I remember when my behavior was questionable my grandmother would wiggle four fingers at me and give me a stark glare. Sometimes, my father tapped the table four times to remind me. When I graduated from college, I saw my mother's

four fingers raised in the crowd.

A stone does not change its color. A stone is firm and solid. You can stand on a stone in the rush of water and not sink. When you acknowledge you are four stones, you will live your life each day reverently with enthusiasm, recognizing your strength and purpose, loving the being you were created. I begin each day looking in the mirror and seeing the person I aspire to be. Wherever I go, I see the possibilities in others I encounter on my life's journey. I wrote this message not for a select group of people but for every person that reads it or hears it: Regardless of your color, your age, whether you are male or female, or your family background. Say to yourself daily,

I am four stones: a child of God, a woman of determination, a credit to my race and an asset to my family and community. Honor that philosophy and proceed forward with dignity.

Being loved for who you are is a remarkable gift.

Examine yourself for the beauty and talent not recognized or compensated by the world. And love the unique being you find within.

-Athelyn Daniel-

ABOUT THE AUTHOR

I am an educator and minister currently living in Arizona. I am married to a patient man who has stood by me as I explore the essence of living. My children enhance my life. They are fulfilling their goals, and my dreams for them. My ministry is to serve and encourage others to improve their lives and communities.

Being loved is a gift.

Love what God created and realize your worth

Starting within yourself

Appreciating the gift of love

Sharing your love as a gift to the world.

Four Stones

Stepping Across Time

BY JOSE MENDOZA

www.ingramcontent.com/pod-product-compliance
Lightning Source LLC
LaVergne TN
LVHW050137080526
838202LV00061B/6504